'They would have a house, a palace, a fortress, a temple, a pantheon where they would be at home, where their parents, the schoolmaster and the priest, those great thwarters of projects, would not be able to poke their noses, where they would be completely free to do all that church, school and family forbade them, that is: forget their manners, go barefoot or in shirt sleeves, or even 'starkers', light fires, boil potatoes, smoke viburnum and above all, hide their buttons and weapons.'

Louis Pergaud, *La Guerre des Boutons (War of the Buttons)*.

In the same series

loft, a style of living, élodie piveteau - caroline wietzel
graffiti, sandrine pereira

© Fitway Publishing, 2005
Original editions in French, English, Spanish, Italian

Translation by Translate-A-Book, Oxford

Design and creation: GRAPH'M/Nord Compo, France

ISBN: 2-7528-0039-8 – Publisher code: T00039 – Copyright registration: April 2005

Printed in Singapore by Tien Wah Press

www.fitwaypublishing.com

Fitway Publishing – 12, avenue d'Italie – 75627 Paris cedex 13, France

archiDesign

cabins
dens and bolt-holes

frank roots

fitway.
publishing

contents

Note:

This book most frequently uses the word 'cabin', a translation of the French 'cabane', meaning a 'small, roughly constructed building', to describe a multitude of temporary structures. This is something more substantial than a simple hut, and is made using a variety of materials. There is no suitable generic term in English.

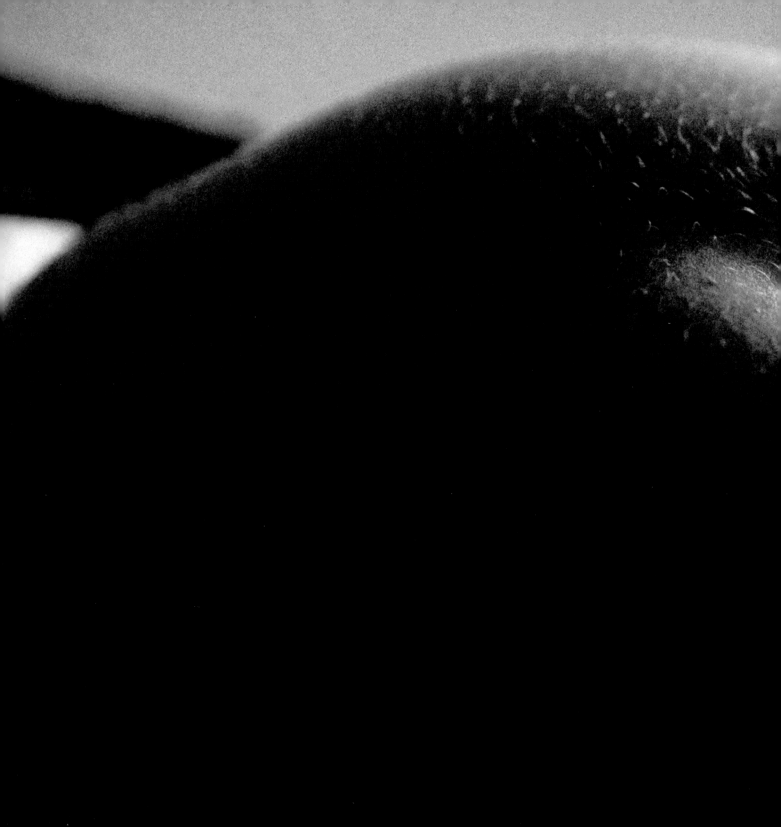

'dad, make

Preceding double page: *Our first cabin. Is this the womb of our fantasies?*

Above: ' ... *a palace, a fortress, a temple, a pantheon where they would be at home, where their parents, [...] those great thwarters of projects, would not be able to poke their noses.' Extract from* La Guerre des Boutons *(War of the Buttons) by Louis Pergaud.*

Right-hand page: *This cabin among the boughs of an Aleppo pine is the refuge of a former publicity agent, Alain Laurens, creator of 'The tree-house' who, for several thousand euros, helps you to make your Robinson dreams come true among the foliage.*

The little prince speaks and, like millions of other fathers all over the world, father gets down to it, not without the occasional pang of nostalgia. Did he not once beg his own father to do the same thing? And without a doubt, his father 'pestered' his grandfather, a long time ago. And so Dad rolls up his sleeves. He is prepared to do it because it doesn't require any superhuman effort and, even if he doesn't have the skill of a master craftsman, no aesthetic judgements can detract from his prestige in the eyes of his child.

In asking for a den, the boy is requesting a further guarantee of the protective capacity of the father: 'Dad, put a roof over my head, you who can do everything.' This is a way of seeking reassurance, a clear confirmation of the father's role. It is a sentiment that the child has difficulty in putting into words, but the simple act of entering into a new den, albeit a modest one, albeit symbolic, will satisfy his need.

me a den!'

Failing to acquiesce to the child's wish would be to risk weakening a relationship of natural trust, and damaging the contract of support that automatically exists between a father or a mother and their child.

This is why, whether in the form of blankets carefully stretched between two chairs (excellent for soothing babies!), branches patiently put together, old boxes, hastily knotted ropes, everyone has undertaken something of the kind at some time with greater or lesser success, launching themselves into the construction of a temporary refuge which is sure to remain engraved as a living memory in the minds of these little adventurers.

A 4,000 square metre (13,000 foot) igloo. Unusual and ephemeral, it is a single-season hotel, built in Sweden using Inuit construction methods. Its doors close in May, when the ice starts to melt!

We build a den or garden cabin for our children and it reminds us of the past. As a recreation of the 'original womb', human beings have experienced such structures throughout their existence, protecting them throughout history, an unceasing progression, renewed from the original cave, whether it is known as a hut, *borie* or *buron*, *sukkot*, caravan, yurt, tepee or wigwam, igloo or Inipi …

In Italy, the monstrous entrance to the caves of the Bosco Sacro (Sacred Woods) **(opposite)**, *sculpted in the 16th century by Count Orsini in his park of Bomarzo, intrigue passers-by, while the caves of the Boboli gardens in Florence have a refreshing feel for visitors.*

Opposite and following double page: *inaccessible cabins for playing 'the Baron in the trees' and escaping ... from parents. When a few metres of height offer the first feelings of freedom ...*

landscape garden

A pavilion designed by painter and lithographer Victor Petit for the Parc de la Motte. (19th century.)

Always utilitarian, it is only recently that these refuges have been given an additional playful dimension with which they are often associated today. Anchored more than ever in the collective imagination, they symbolise a certain liberty, an assertion of contempt for the constraints of the everyday. They bring together two definite values of our time, here at the beginning of the 21st century: a return to nature, and nostalgia. This explains their popularity. There are countless exhibitions, publications and websites devoted to them.

They give full rein to the imagination of landscape gardeners. We are seeing tribute paid once again to follies and *fabriques*[1], with a renewed increase in their importance in parks and gardens. They inspire gardeners' fantasies: no major public horticultural exhibition is now complete without a display of these little buildings in living, woven wickerwork, which were popular as far back as medieval times.

Right-hand page: *The temple of Sybille, a Tivoli replica, dominates the park of Buttes-Chaumont in Paris. It is reached via a path punctuated by suspended bridges, waterfalls and artificial grottoes.*

They are a source of reflection for contemporary designers. For example, they have become a kind of portable arbour in the imaginations of brothers Erwan and Ronan Bouroullec *(p. 22-23)*, although in such designs they display very few of the main characteristics of the roughly built cabin, which should be an assembly of materials found on site (wood and leaves in forests, dry stones on bare land, discarded objects and found materials in an urban environment).

Above: *The Carré Rouge by Gloria Friedmann is an installation in France, on the shore of a lake on the Langres plateau. The comfort it offers is spartan, but the concealed façade is fully glazed and open to nature. It is a hiker's refuge available for hire, but the waiting list is long.*

Right-hand page, top: *A blue cube on a green carpet, in the Bagatelle park.*

Right-hand page, bottom: *Autocrat, by the Atelier Van Lieshout.*

This betrayal is rejected by Joep Van Lieshout, founder of the Atelier of the same name (opposite) who, more in the spirit of the tradition, undertakes to design cabins made from corrugated metal sheets, tarpaulins, old cardboard boxes, etc.

Cabins inspire artists such as Daniel Buren, creator of the Cabane éclatée (Exploded cabin) (1990–1991), an installation comprising a timber structure reminiscent of the skeleton of a small half-timbered house.

Some pieces of tarpaulin (striped of course, the artists's signature!) are stretched between the vertical posts; others are fixed to the walls of the room the eye falls on first. In the same series the artist also presented a work called *Cabane éclatée deux fois (Cabin exploded twice)*. This work has the addition of a set of mirrors that reflect, inside the structure, the image of the visitor, who thus sees himself as part of the cabin: a striking way of placing the spectator within the work of art, but also a visual creation of the situation of the 'cabin man', a virtual inhabitant of the ephemeral.

Above: *Adults can be big children. The Red Cell advertising agency offices, created by Matali Crasset (2001).*

Opposite: *The* Cabane *is a perfect illustration of the minimalist style of brothers Ronan and Erwan Bouroullec.*

A sense of provocation is also found in the work of Jean-François Fourtou who, with *Singe (Monkey)* (2003), creates a playful, ambiguous work: a small cabin is made using a table, folded mattresses, a large box, a stepladder and draped curtains, but a large red-haired fake fur monkey is leaving the scene, a pillow and a chair under his arm. A poetic return to the primitive cabin born of the subconscious mind of an artist.

Above: *Within its structure, which has all the appearance of an impermeable storage cupboard, the* Lounge mobile *by Kasane conceals a lounge on wheels with adjustable feet enabling it to be adapted to suit all kinds of floor.*

Opposite: *The international New York architects Asymptote have conceived a veritable office-cocoon (for Knoll International).*

Above: *For the exterior, a cabin/store/veranda by Erwan and Ronan Bouroullec.*

Right-hand page: *The Paper Loghouse by Japanese architect Shigeru Ban was constructed in 1995 to house Japanese victims of the Kobe earthquake. Fire resistant and resting on crates of beer cans filled with sand, its walls are made of cardboard tubes, and its roof of insulating textile.*

The cabin also inspires the creativity of various contemporary architects who see this return to basics as a source of renewed dynamism. In this they are followers in the footsteps of their great *sachem*, Le Corbusier who, in the 1950s; was seeking to achieve legitimacy for the new principles that he wanted to see prevailing. He had the idea of constructing a beach hut on a promontory of rocks beaten by the waves, between Menton and Monaco. 'I have a castle on the Côte d'Azur,' he said, 'measuring 3.66 metres by 3.66 metres (12 feet by 12 feet). It's for my wife, an extravagance of comfort, of nobility.' A very modest castle: planks, a door, a window, and that's all. People used to value, they still value, experience: the slightest assembly of logs counts if it is put together by an architect respected by those at the forefront in his profession. Hence, cohorts of architecture students from all over the world come to see Le Corbusier's structure. However, despite its practical details, its 'principles of layout[2]', its integration into the environment – and even if this tiny creation was the shelter to which the great man of Art regularly retreated over more than 18 years to invent an alternative architecture for the world – we are entitled to think (without wishing to cause any offence!) that, 50 years later, Le Corbusier's cabin has lost its soul: a cabin has less meaning as an industrious assemblage than as the expression by an individual or a group of a desire to be different.

from cave to

Above: *The tree: I am the wood of which cabins are made … immortalised in the Georges Brassens song.*

Right-hand page: *Shiny and polished like shell cases, the Airstream trailers which once flowed along the American highways are in decline.*

But let us return to the primitive cabin and push a door open: at the dawn of time, the cabin was invented by man as a shelter from the weather and for protection from predators. But straight away this gave rise to a worrying paradox: designed for the comfort and well-being of individuals, it was born of the irresistible urge of men to be on the move, to travel and to discover the world. It must have beer the possibility of hunting over greater and greater distances without having to return to the family cave every evening which led him to devise his first refuge, by climbing a tree, then arranging a few branches to provide cover. Eugène Viollet-le-Duc, architect of the neo-Gothic generation in France, describes the scene in his *Histoire de l'Habitation Humaine Depuis les Temps Préhistoriques Jusqu'à nos Jours (History of Human Habitation from Prehistoric Times to the Present)*, published in 1875[3]: 'Epergos chose two young trees a few paces apart. Hoisting himself up into one of them, he caused it to bend under the weight of his body, reached out for the top of the other using a hooked stick and, thus bringing the branches of the two trees together, tied them in place using rushes.' One can imagine that, the next morning, the modest structure was abandoned and just a few days later, nature had removed all traces of the passage of men, as if she suspected all the wrongs that this formidable race would cause her in the future.

mobile home

This is an early mention of the ephemerality of the cabin (from the Greek *ephemeros*, 'which only lasts one day') which appears to be one of the basic conditions that apply to, indeed are necessary for, its existence.

Down the centuries, the complexity of structures has increased but, for a number of thinkers, from Vitruvius of Rome (circa 50 BC) to Édouard Jeanneret-Gris, known as Le Corbusier, through Marc-Antoine Laugier and Eugène Viollet-le-Duc, the cabin would be at the heart of the architectural creation. This theory is currently popular but fiercely opposed by (a minority of) other theoreticians and art historians, essentially for the reasons given above: the cabin is not made to last.

Certain discoveries support this standpoint. In France, at Arcy-sur-Cure in Burgundy, a number of substructures were found dating from the Upper Palaeolithic era (before 35,000 BC), showing that buildings already existed at that time, made from mammoth tusks and slabs. Evidence of this kind of structure had already been found in Ukraine and southern Russia. These structures could sometimes require the killing of about a hundred mammoths and were not intended to be portable. These characteristics made them residences in the true sense of the word, which cabins are not.

If a number of architects persist with the myth of the primitive cabin, the symbol of the state of nature

so dear to Jean-Jacques Rousseau, is it not because it represents all that architecture no longer is, fully immersed as it is in a society where liberty, poetry and profitability rarely sit happily side by side?

Let us note here that in the case of the architect/artist Guy Rottier[4], things seem to have come full circle and extremes are reconciled. He is one of those who, in their works, make sense of structure and utopia, using unexpected materials that give their projects the fragile and ephemeral appearance of

(genuine) cabins. His cardboard villages, his architecture of the earth, his solar house, his suspended holiday homes[5] and his immovable rocks make reference to caves and troglodyte homes, never losing sight of the poetic ideal of the original cabin. But it is above all his snail house (built on the basis of a central section made of local stone, leading to a helical design radiating out in stages as the family grows) which is the most obvious reference.

His creations illustrate a possible parallel development of the ephemeral cabin and more permanent architecture – just as the two species of man, Neanderthal and Cro-Magnon, coexisted and developed independently 50,000 years ago. A bold comparison, but not too far-fetched if one considers that one of the two groups, the Neanderthals, died out (the ephemeral), leaving the world in the hands of the Cro-Magnons (our true ancestors).

Preceding double page: *As with cabins, from time immemorial people have loved to enter grottoes with a primitive feeling, often mixed with apprehension, of getting close to nature.*

Urban gardeners of today do not grow things because of need, but for pleasure. Rows of allotments and their corrugated metal cabins are an image of past times.

Let us delve a little deeper into the motivations of these 'grown-up children': this nest, for that is certainly what it is, has the quality of a refuge, of a place to rest. Returning to the nest is to return to the security of one's first home, and to the sense of well-being which followed birth. As the philosopher Gaston Bachelard said: 'In essence, all life is well-being. The being begins with well-being.'

But let us not forget that the nest, with its qualities of peace and 'snuggling up', is also the symbol of taking a giant leap and flying away … which leaves us reassured: a tree house is not merely a return to childhood, but is also a way of gaining height in order to spread your wings and take flight!

The 'Robinson cabins', which for a long time were the Sunday retreats of pleasure-seeking Parisians, clearly belong to the category of 'cabin of dreams'/ tree house. In the 19th century, Joseph Guesquin, a keen reader of *The Swiss Family Robinson* by J. D. Wyss, published in 1813[7], encountered the locality of La Châtaigneraie, near to Le Plessis, a few kilometres from the capital, which had huge trees. He immediately decided to install some wood cabins linked by a staircase between the largest of them, and to establish a restaurant there under the name of the *Grand Robinson*. Instant success. Other restaurateurs soon imitated him. These *guinguettes* in the trees of the Plessis-Robinson district became popular places to visit and were known far and wide. A chronicler of the age described the atmosphere which prevailed here thus: 'It is neither a village nor a hamlet, but one huge open-air restaurant, quiet during the week, but extraordinarily lively on Sundays. At Robinson, there is feasting in all the trees, people drinking on all the terraces and beneath all the arbours, there is dancing on all the lawns.

A little garden shed and planted plots in the garden of Acclimatation in Paris.

From Sceaux, from Fontenay, from all the surrounding areas, people arrive in charabancs, in cars, on horseback, by donkey, on foot, in long lines, in serried ranks, with whetted appetites and songs on their lips[8].'

Cabins of freedom. These are made for children who dream of imitating adults enjoying the freedom of doing anything they please, and in particular doing that which is forbidden to them (see the quotation earlier from *La Guerre des Boutons (War of the Buttons)*, by Louis Pergaud, *see page 2*). A desire for freedom which, four centuries before the birth of Christ, inspired Diogenes the cynic who, from the heart of his arbour (his cabin!), scorned convention and social constraints and abandoned himself to all kinds of eccentricity. The complete deprivation experienced by the Greek philosopher and the modesty of his shelter demanded respect and protected him from the law.

Opposite: *Cabins in the trees are currently the subject of a flourishing trade. These days, anyone can construct their cabin according to principles and using materials that have no regard to the integrity nor the health of the tree. Here, the Cabane perchée, erected by a group of friends in the Lubéron region.*

Right-hand page: *The owner of this former tool shed thought big; by adding a terrace, he has transformed it into a palace*

fortune

The concept of the *emergency cabin* was born in 1942, in the United States. This was a house for the homeless, made from fibreboard and costing 50 dollars. One hour was all it took to assemble the 21 panels from which it was made. Its resistance to the wind and rain was remarkable.

Some years later, in 1954, during a particularly harsh winter, France had to tackle the same problem. The bombings of the Second World War had thrown millions of people out onto the streets, and these had found refuge in shelters made of bits and pieces, but above all from old fuel cans *(bidons)* abandoned by the liberation forces. These settlements, known as *bidonvilles*, had become features of the outskirts of all the major conurbations.

Left-hand page: *A temporary cabin, an absurd shelter against the Moscow cold.*

Above: *This is art.* La Favela Beach House *is an installation by the Atelier Van Lieshout, inspired by the shanties of the homeless.*

Nine years later, despite the substantial efforts which had already been made towards reconstruction, there were still many people living in unacceptable conditions. This is why Abbé Pierre, founder of the Emmaus movement, launched an appeal to resolve the problems of the homeless and established collections to enable the construction of new dwellings. An architect with a social conscience, Jean Prouvé, sought solutions to alleviate the state of emergency and came up with a system of small dwellings, 6 metres by 6 metres, which could be erected in one day.

Today, 50 years later, the problem of the homeless has still not been fully solved. Millions of people around the world still live on the streets, and then there are those who are victims of wars or natural disasters. So there will always be a need for such emergency cabins.

Above: *Winter 1954. Abbé Pierre founded the Companions of Emmaus to offer aid to the homeless and to provide them with more effective shelters against the cold than those plank cabins which characterised the suburbs of the major French cities.*

Right-hand page: *This Favela House is a creation of the Atelier Van Lieshout. These artists, as others, wished to contribute their statement in the fight against precariousness.*

Against the background of the tragic civil war and genocide in Rwanda, followed by the earthquake disaster in Kobe, Japan, the Japanese architect Shigeru Ban took the American idea of the fibre-board cabin and designed a cardboard house which could be erected quickly – the 'Paper Loghouse' – placed on crates of sand-filled bottles *(see p. 27)*. As durable as the container-type temporary homes or prefabricated shelters, but costing much less, Shigeru Ban's cabins are better insulated, against both cold and heat, and easy to recycle.

Above: *Joep Van Lieshout defines his work as 'art to be used'. His installations (here, in Barcelona) have the benefit of attracting attention and triggering the right kinds of questions.*

Right-hand page: *In the suburbs of Rio, in Brasil, there is no question of beauty to ameliorate poverty; just a heaped collection of favelas.*

In Saharan Africa, there are no demands but a single priority: to provide impermeability against sand storms.

Cabins of protest. A new concept, still in its infancy. Protest cabins have appeared with the rise of the ecological movement, and have proved ideal for symbolising the defence of the environment, demonstrating against the chosen route of a motorway, the siting of a nuclear power station or even a high-voltage power line. In 2004, the centuries-old oaks of the forest of Ferney-Voltaire, in the Ain region, which were threatened with being felled to assure the security of the airport at Geneva, although 15 kilometres away[9], became filled with tree houses (containing protestors!); they were very modest structures, but perfect for gaining the sympathies of the public for the protest movement and for keeping at bay the lumberjacks and their chainsaws brought in from outside (the local lumberjacks did not want to get their hands dirty on this tainted project).

A fare on a lagoon ... This image has contributed substantially to the dreamlike attraction exercised by Polynesia. However, they are often utilitarian structures.

functional

More than tents, caravans have for a long time been the ultimate *nomads' cabins*. They are rarely seen on the roads these days, and have been replaced by mobile homes or the modern caravans of holidaymakers. But, whether Dutch, Irish, the typical two-coloured caravans of the Camargue, or the decorative wooden gypsy caravans, they continue to symbolise a certain kind of travelling. They can be hired for a week's or fortnight's holiday spent exploring the quiet byways and canal towpaths, discovering an unknown land – even if it's in one's own country. You don't live in a caravan, you travel in it. The bed is on the floor, in an alcove separated by a sliding door, and the furniture is light enough to be removed and replaced easily in the case of emergencies. Living in a caravan forces us to distinguish between what is necessary and what is superfluous; the absence of home comforts is a low price to pay for the feeling of 'completeness' rediscovered, according to all reports. The caravan is a philosophy of life.

Preceding double page: *These cabins on wheels are the contemporary habitat of nomadic peoples, direct descendants of the gypsy caravans of former times that travelled the dusty lanes.*

Opposite: *In the 15th century, an Andalusian shepherd discovered a statue of the Virgin in the Guadalquivir marshes. Since that time, once a year, thousands of men and women in traditional costume undertake an eight-day pilgrimage and festival. This is the Rocio, one of the most extravagant pilgrimages in the world.*

Utilitarian cabins. There are still many cabins today which serve a practical purpose, even if associations of 'leisure' are never too far away: we are not speaking here of site huts, charmless boxes erected close to building sites, but rather those used to house the equipment necessary for fishing or bathing by the sea, or hunting accessories in the forests. In gardens they become repositories for tools, and at lakesides, boathouses. Camouflaged in the trees, they make perfect look-out posts. They are given a huge variety, ad infinitum, of specific uses: retreats for reading, model-making, contemplation, painting, poetry, taking afternoon tea – Queen Victoria had one erected at the top of a tree specifically for this purpose[10]! … Whatever their intended purpose, they all offer their occupants, often solitary, the opportunity to withdraw from the everyday, to replenish themselves, to find moments for dreaming or escaping into the realm of the imagination.

In the estuary of the Gironde, many of these carrelets did not stand up to the heavy storms of the late 20th century.

This shelter is an island between sky and water.

*These dry-stone shepherds' huts are found along the lanes of the south
of France. Here, near Gordes.*

The freedom they imply goes as far as breaking away from the slightest reference to any particular style of decoration. Thus, with reference to the Marseille *cabanons* (former fishermen's huts whose prices are escalating on the leisure-oriented property market), Xavier Girard, art historian, emphasised: 'People don't make any extra 'effort', any concession to home interior aesthetics; they recycle discarded furniture, making a complete confusion of genres and styles. Here, nothing could be more irrelevant than bad taste, kitsch horrors, general impurity. The idiom is reuse, ingenious or 'artistic' DIY, sparseness, impurity, a composite, a kaleidoscope of tastes. The heterogeneity of the 'experience' in miniature separates the cabin from any particular dictates of style[11] … ' This is a 'non-style' which delights the readers of home and interior design magazines. It is an example of recuperation in all senses of the word.

Mounted high on stilts for hunting turtle doves in the woods of the Gironde **(left-hand page)**, *or half buried like the palombières of the Landes* **(above)** *for hunting wood pigeons, these huntsmen's structures represent tradition … and the art of waiting.*

It seems unclear whether 'utilitarian' or 'leisure' best describes the *palombières* in the trees of the forests of the Landes region, from which the hunters of pigeons watch for their prey; the subterranean *tonnes* of Bordeaux from where unwary ducks are shot; or the *carrelets*, fishermen's huts on stilts constructed in lines on the shores of the Gironde or the coast of Charente-Maritime; or the *tchanqué* cabins on stilts of the Bassin d'Arcachon, once used by oyster farmers to oversee their oyster beds; many of these have become very expensive holiday chalets.

In France impeccable rows of beach huts line the coast, made from wood or from canvas, immutably striped as if from the last century.

Beach huts, holiday cabins.

Opposite, above and following double page: *With their bright colours or pastel shades, the famous huts of the coastguards, those great swimmers and lifesavers, adorn the American beaches.*

Cabins at risk. With the disappearance of certain jobs, or, more prosaically, with the multiplication of means of transport, certain kinds of utilitarian cabin are faced with extinction, or have already disappeared completely from the countryside. These include the charcoal-burners' or foresters' huts *(loges)*, the *cabanons* of the tappers who collected the resin from the pines of the Landes. Or the *baraquettes* of the Sète region, originally for housing agricultural workers, which became meeting places for eating, drinking and singing in short, partying – there is even an expression in the local dialect: *'mettre chichois en baraquette'* (like a reveller in the *baraquette*, which means, roughly, 'creating havoc', or, more coloquially, 'like a bull in a china shop'. In terms of its use, the Sétois *baraquette* (which has almost disappeared) was the Languedoc cousin of the Corsican *paillotes* (still going strong!), the temporary restaurants on the coast, which disappear in the autumn (at least in theory).

If certain types of cabin survive, it is often because they are made of solid material; this is true of the winegrowers' or shepherds' cabins constructed of dry stones carefully arranged to form a vaulted structure. They were intended as overnight refuges when the workplace was far away from the home and they have lasted down the years, surviving bad weather and predators (walkers, penniless masons,

scavengers of building materials, etc.). The builders of these stone huts had no choice: there was no timber available on the limestone plateaux where the vines were grown or sheep grazed – but there was plenty of stone. The construction technique was incredibly simple: relatively flat stones piled up in a circle.

The walls inclined inwards and met at the top, with a hole left for smoke to escape. In winter a fire would be lit inside, and the stones of the walls absorbed the heat, then radiated it back: veritable storage heaters. A low door, always facing away from the prevailing winds, was the means of access.

In Galicia, in the north-west of Spain, the Hórreos are still to be found, cabin-silos for storing provisions. Dubbed 'granaries on stilts', they are raised on rough columns or piles to keep animals from climbing in.

As the phylloxera vine disease swept through the vine-yards at the end of the 19th century, these shelters were abandoned at the same time as the vines and, nature having reasserted itself, it is not uncommon to come across them hidden in the undergrowth, invaded by vegetation, defying time.

Left-hand page: *The adobe hogans of the Indians of the south seem to have grown out of the ground.*

Above: *The Apaches used flexible poles covered with grass, bark and brushwood. The hogan was burned when its occupant died.*

Local oral legend often attributes ages of 500 years to them, although it appears that the ones found in the French regions are no more than 200 to 250 years old. But this is an eternity in cabin terms!

Their names are regional; they are called *bories* throughout most of France, *bordes, capitelles* in the Gard and Hérault regions, *gariottes* and *caselles* in Dordogne and Quercy, *orries* in the *département* of

Pyrénées-Orientales, *chibottes* in the Velay, *cadoles* in Mâconnais, *barracuns* and *paillers* in Corsica, etc. And let us leave the list there, but not before mentioning the *talayots* of the Balearics, the Sardinian *nuraghi* and the *trullis* of Puglia in southern Italy, constructed according to the same principles and devoted to the same uses.

Cabins of memory. Cabins are places of passing through; they may also be the embodiment of a memory, as symbolised by the sukkah booths celebrated in Jewish festival, which are traditionally reconstructed every year, in memory of the 40 years spent in these makeshift shelters in the desert. These rustic shelters that could house the whole family are also a celebration of nature. If possible, four species of tree should be used in their construction: the palm, the ultimate desert tree; the willow, which grows along watercourses and is a reminder of the crossing of the Jordan; the myrtle, which is found in the mountainous regions like those around Bethlehem and Jericho; and finally, the citron of the coastal plains.

Left-hand page: *It is said that during the gold rush, the real 'winners' were those who constructed cabins to provide food and lodgings for the prospectors, and to sell them shovels and pickaxes (here, on the banks of Lake Laberge). Fortunately timber was not as rare as the precious metal.*

Above: *Immortalised for eternity, these plains Indians pose outside their home ... without knowing that, a hundred and fifty years later, 'authentic' tepees would be available to all on the Internet, made to measure, for a few thousand dollars.*

At the beginning of the last century, Alphonse Levy, an Alsatian painter of Jewish life, described the festive atmosphere which reigned during the days of the Sukkotfestival: 'Men, young people, children, everyone worked on the sukkah (the booth). In every courtyard, on every street corner, in all the little squares, rustic shelters for the whole family were erected. Four solid posts, planted firmly in the ground, form the foundations for these open-air huts. The ornamentation of the booth is firmly fixed by tradition. Blue and yellow paper chains are draped alongside wild rose branches with their red hips, standing out beautifully against the greenery. Affixed to the trellis are all the fruits of the season: pears, apples, grapes, nuts. Finally, not far from the door, majestically balanced – and indispensable, infallible protection against all influence of evil – is a glorious red onion, decorated with colourful cockerel feathers.'

For seven days, the sukkat has to replace the home. The family must eat, read and meet with friends under its roof. Once the festival is over, it will disappear, to be reborn next time.

Lodge hotel for wealthy tourists. African adventure meets western comfort.

the cabin

# of dreams

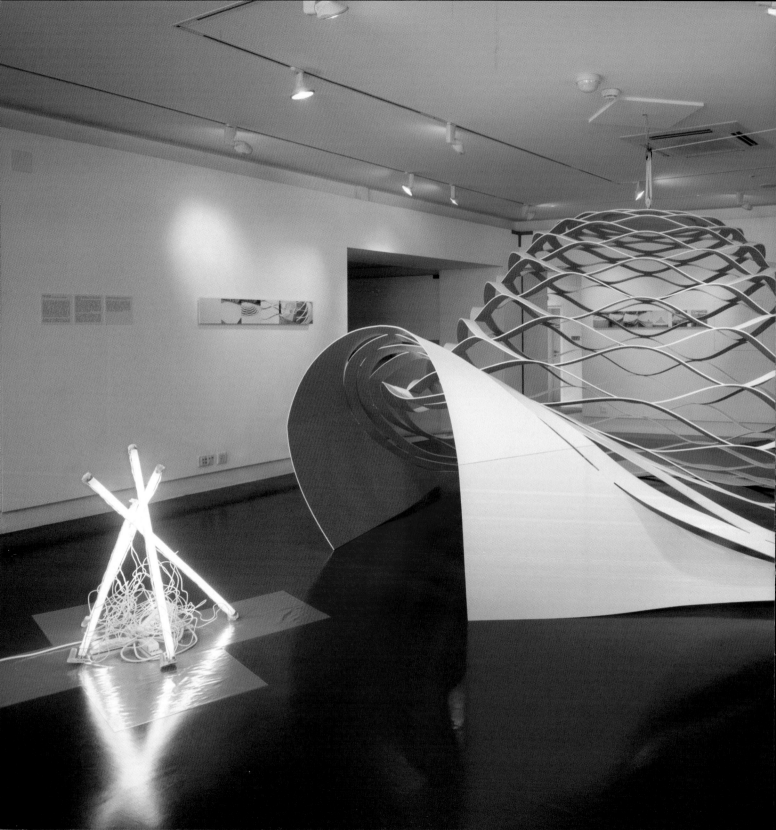

Cabins haunt our nights just as they form part of our memories. It often happens that one appears in a dream. It is empty, usually uninhabited, and most frequently made of wood. But, in fact, is it a cabin or something simpler? The question is important as, although similar in terms of representation and both expressing a primitive need to return to childhood, they have complex functions in dream interpretation, and fundamentally different symbolic values. Also, statistics show that men generally conjure up well-constructed cabins, while women more frequently dream of simple huts.

In his impressive work *Dictionnaire de la Symbolique (Dictionary of Symbolism)*[12], Georges Romey gives guidelines on finding the correct name to be applied to the 'temporary and precarious' structure that the dreamer encounters on his or her path. In dreams, the hut of women's imaginations most frequently appears with exotic décor, in a tropical environment. If it had a host, this would be Robinson Crusoe.

Preceding double page: *In the Parc de la Villette, a folly by Bernard Tschumi* **(left-hand page)**. *The interior of a lodge in Zimbabwe* **(right-hand page)**.

Opposite: *Matali Crasset cultivates the art of skilful cutting out. How a two-dimensional mat can be made into a 'habitable' cabin.*

At home with designer Azzedine Alaia. A former filling station by Jean Prouvé has metamorphosed into a bedroom.

The anti-loft, or how architecture revived the principle of the Russian doll.

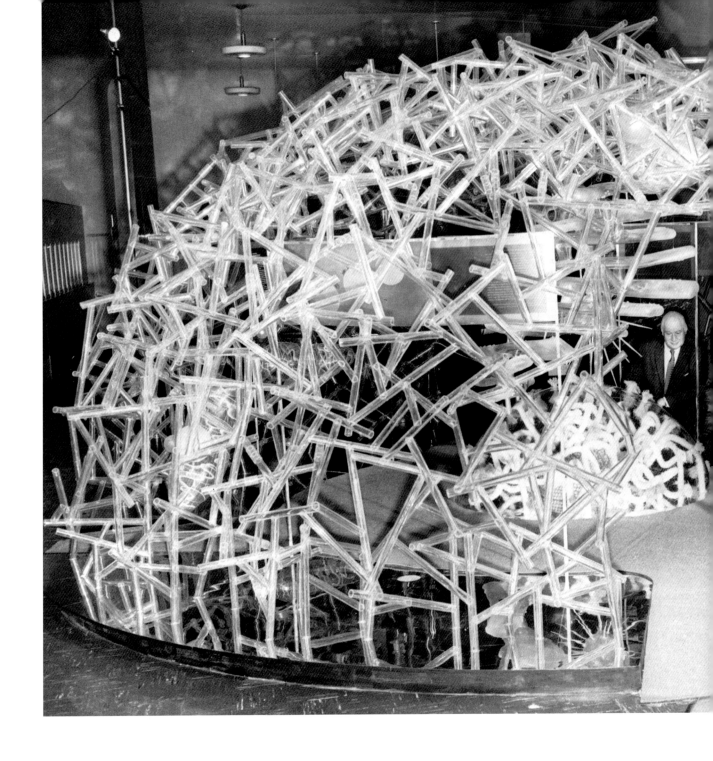

The cabin, on the other hand, could be the home of a trapper – perhaps Davy Crockett, to stay with the childish imagery? 'It belongs to the most septentrional strata of the imagination,' Georges Romey states, adding: 'The mode of expression of the dreamer who conjures up this symbol is characterised by seriousness, an embodiment of gravity.' The climate, the environment and the atmosphere of the place are what essentially make the difference. 'The cabin is a place of welcome, providing both food and restorative function, where substantial nourishment will be lavished upon those who know how to receive it … Appearing in the fruit of the masculine imagination more frequently than in scenarios produced by female dreamers, the cabin, in the vocabulary of images, is a word representing a movement towards the rehabilitation of the *anima*[13].'

With regard to the simple hut dreamt of by women, Romey adds: 'Encountering this symbol in a dream is to release oneself from the excesses of reasoning in which a being is led astray. In the vocabulary of images, the hut is an antonym of the labyrinth. The latter denotes the trap that is set by the network of intellectual justifications.

By magnifying a blood cell a million times, visionary architect Richard Buckminster Fuller (on the right), created the geodesic dome, one of the most solid structures known in relation to the weight of the materials used.

Inflatable frameworks, by the Inflate collective.

The hut takes the dreamer back to the early dawn of infancy, to a time when the collective values of the subconscious had not yet been sacrificed in favour of the structuring of the conscious ego.'

Men dream of cabins for the same reasons as they build them: they find in them a remedy for the complexities of the world.

This dream was lived out 'for real' by Henry David Thoreau, American essayist, who, at the beginning of the 19th century, undertook to live alone for two years in a cabin in the depths of the forest in Massachusetts. He published an account of his experience in 1854 in *Walden; or Life in the Woods*. Ascetic, naturalist and poet, Thoreau's motto was: 'Simplify, simplify'. But his objective was not to change society – as was the case for those who rediscovered him in the 1960s, during the global protest movement that swept through the Western world, particularly among students – but to live an intense personal experience, to lead a meditative life and to resist the dictates of organised society; to rid himself of hopes, aspirations, to live in harmony with nature 'giving himself up to universal gravitation'.

The Lit clos, created by the Bouroullec brothers for Capellini. Partway between Californian coastguard hut and the traditional Breton bed, it is a contemporary response in aluminium, steel and lacquered wood to the growing number of people who live, work and sleep in the same space.

'I turned my face more exclusively than ever to the woods.'

Installing himself in his cabin on the edges of Walden pond, whose waters he compared to those of the Ganges, and whose countryside to the steppes of Tartary, Henry David Thoreau said that he touched 'harmony', a harmony which he translated into simple words:

'To anticipate, not the sunrise and the dawn merely, but, if possible, Nature herself!'

'For many years I was self-appointed inspector of snow-storms and rain-storms ... '

'Trying to hear what was in the wind'

'To stand on the meeting of two eternities, the past and future, which is precisely the present moment; to toe that line.'

A garden in a cabin. The Meuble-jardin by Vincent Dupont-Rougier and Patrick Nadeau produced under the patronage of the Maison Hermès opens up on four sides, revealing a conservatory, an extension made of extendable cross-pieces, and a terrace for contemplation and resting.

Abandoned for more than 150 years, Thoreau's cabin is still standing and open to visitors. In *Lent dehors*[14], novelist Philippe Djian describes the pilgrimage he made to the place, and his sense of deception when he discovered that civilisation, with the laudable intention of preservation, had to all intents and purposes killed the myth. 'Between the car park and the main road, on a strip of land a few metres wide, surrounded by rubbish bins, was Thoreau's cabin. Or rather its exact replica, perfect down to the last detail, as described on the sign – apart from the fact that it had been moved half a mile from the location of the original, for the purposes of the highways authorities. Rather like a little doll's house … '

The Walden cabin did indeed exist, but does so no longer, like all the cabins invented by literature, those of all the Robinsons and adventurers down the ages.

They often provide a shelter for voluntary solitude conducive to meditation, verging on misanthropy.

In collaboration with Jorge Orta, Lucy Orta conceived the **Refuge Wear-Habitent,** *multipurpose garments which can be transformed into survival tents. Her ambition is to provoke thought on the deprivations in our society (poverty, lack of security), and to offer, at least symbolically (her garments are prototypes) emergency solutions for certain situations such as natural disasters.*

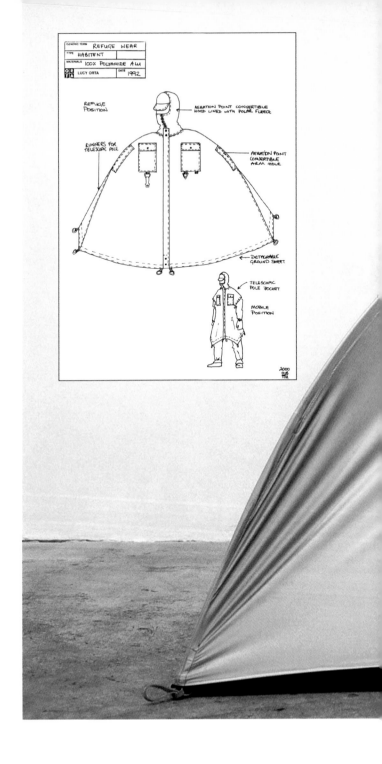

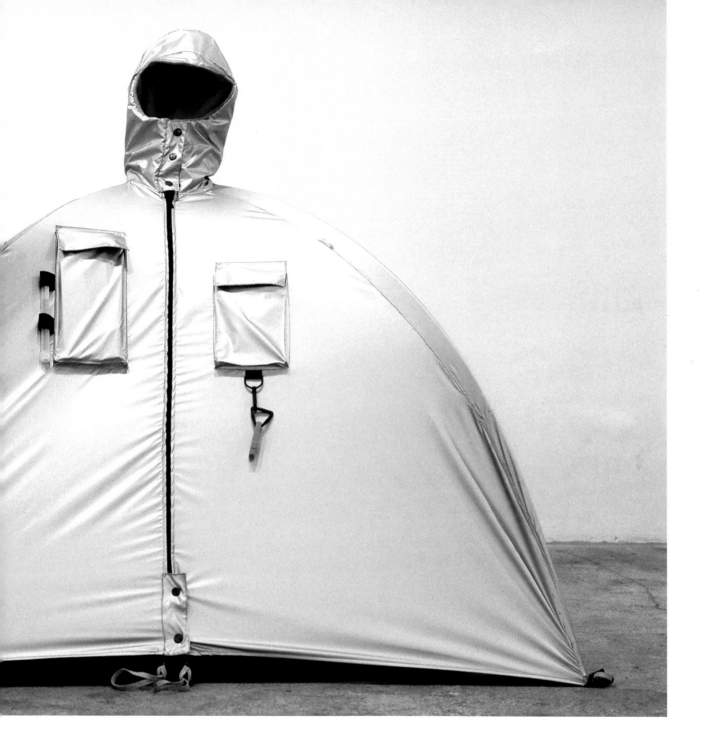

Opposite: *From Matali Cresset's Oritapi (combining rug [tapis] and origami), a tepee is born.*

Above: *Fairytales are full of cabins that are enticing yet contain hidden dangers. Here, children can relive the adventures of Hansel and Gretel while playing ice-cream stand.*

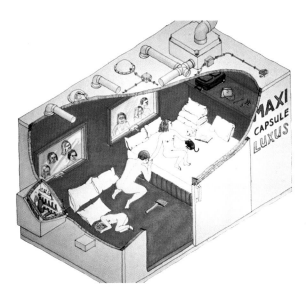

Thoreau confesses: 'I love to be alone. I never found the companion that was so companionable as solitude. We are for the most part more lonely when we go abroad among men than when we stay in our chambers.' The cabin is comfortable with company and visitors. Its destiny at Walden was to be ephemeral. This is true of all cabins, as we have seen.

The Dutch artists of the Atelier Van Lieshout reinvent surroundings for sexual pleasures, such as the Bais-O-Drome (opposite), a 'bubble' produced in 1995, and the Maxi Capsule Luxus (above).

More traditional, the STAR wagon by the same Atelier Van Lieshout is contained in a former railway carriage. A 33 square metre (108 square foot) cabin on wheels.

Notes

page 18: 1. Follies were pavilions built purely for amusement in the parklands of stately homes, very fashionable in the 17th and 18th centuries. *Fabriques* were small decorative buildings, which often had philosophical significance. Some of them also had a useful purpose: ice houses, stores, etc. These structures often imitated ruins. Their main objective was to surprise, but also to stimulate passers-by to reflect. They fell out of fashion in the upheaval of the French Revolution.

page 26: 2. The measurements are directly linked to human dimensions. Its height of 2.26 metres, for example, is the average height of a man with an arm raised.

page 28: 3. Eugène Viollet-le-Duc, *Histoire de l'Habitation Humaine Depuis les Temps Préhistoriques Jusqu'à Nos Jours*.

Page 30: 4. 'With all my creations I have sought to guess or divine the future, like a painter, sculptor or designer. I want to uproot people, to prove to them that there are ways and unimagined byways to be discovered. I love the unrivalled Gothic cathedrals, that certain something of Cheval, Gaudi, Le Corbusier, beauty and ugliness. Architecture invents itself! Architecture should be free, because it is a constantly evolving art. A necessary condition to enable creation and tradition to meet!' Guy Rottier, Frac Centre (Centre Regional Contemporary Art Fund), 1999.

page 31: 5. Types of caravans suspended from a network of cables. Instead of being fixed in one location, they can easily be moved, then, at the end of the season, be taken under cover and detached during the winter.

page 36: 6. These cost between 30,000 and 60,000 euros in 2005.

page 39: 7. Johann David Wyss, *The Swiss Family Robinson*.

page 40: 8. Alexis Martin, *Les Étapes d'un Touriste en France* (1894) Nîmes, C. Lacour, coll. 'Redivia', 2002.

page 49: 9. A security-related version of the old saying: 'If you want to kill your dog accuse it of having rabies.' Getting rid of 3,500 trees in order to ensure the security of Geneva airport was a dubious argument. According to the protestors (including almost all the residents of Fernay-Voltaire united against their mayor!), this was really a matter of developing commercial property and opening up the possibility for the airport to expand more easily in future!

page 55: 10. Different again from the Canadian 'sugar shacks' where, in season (called the 'sugar season', generally from 1 March to 1 May), happy groups of people get together at the heart of the maple groves of Quebec to taste, among other things, the *tire sur la neige*, hot maple syrup drizzled over snow.

page 59: 11. '*La lézarde du monde*' (The lizard of the world), by Xavier Girard, in *La Pensée de Midi*, n° 11, a quarterly magazine published by Actes Sud.

page 77: 12. Georges Romey, *Dictionnaire de la Symbolique. Le vocabulaire fondamental des rêves (Dictionary of Symbolism. The fundamental vocabulary of dreams)*.

page 83: 13. The *anima*, according to Carl Gustav Jung, is the subconscious feminine aspect that every man carries inside himself. For anyone who wants to progress in personal development, it is essential to objectivise within him the efficiencies of the *anima*, in order to discover the psychic content at the origin of the mysterious efficiencies of the soul. The more the relationship between the ego and the *anima* becomes intimate and personal, the better.

page 90: 14. Philippe Djian *Lent dehors*, Bernard Barrault, Paris, 1991.

cabin is ... ∎ ... ∎

- a machine for dreaming, an image factory, something fragile, composite and intimate ...
- a desire to live differently in the world ...
- a means of distancing yourself from reality, of withdrawing, or obtaining a higher perspective, of dreaming ...
- a refuge on a human scale, where you feel protected and to which you can retire, find your inner self ...
- a dream for getting back in touch with your emotions, feelings and the games of childhood ...
- a place to meditate, create, read, write, dream, imagine, draw, paint, make music ...
- the means of getting back in touch with the rhythms of nature, of regaining contact with the world of living things ...
- a way of giving back a human dimension to our living spaces ...
- an invitation to build, and to reconstruct yourself.

Cabins should disappear quickly and if they prevent the inevitable, if they petrify them at a certain moment of their disintegration, people do them infinite harm.
A cabin continues to live once it has disappeared, and dies as it continues to exist.

bibliography

The major classics ...

Daniel Defoe: *Robinson Crusoe* (Oxford Paperbacks, 1998).
In *Émile, ou Traité de l'Éducation*, Jean-Jacques Rousseau recommended this work to Émile, in preference even to Aristotle, Pliny or Buffon.

Louis Pergaud: *La Guerre des Boutons [War of the Buttons]* (Gallimard Jeunesse, 2003).
The Longevernes versus the Velrans: a timeless history of rivalry between the children of neighbouring villages in which the cabin has an important role as the nerve centre of 'military operations'.

Jules Verne: *The Mysterious Island* (Random House USA Inc., 2004), *Adrift in the Pacific – Two Years Holiday* (Fredonia Books, 2003), and *Uncle Robinson*, a manuscript not published in the author's lifetime, but later published by Le Cherche Midi (Paris, 1991) (not translated into English). How to survive in a hostile environment thanks to science and natural resources.

Robert-Louis Stevenson: *Travels with a Donkey in the Cevennes* (Penguin classics, 2003).

Crossing the Cevennes with a donkey, in the autumn of 1878, by the author of *Treasure Island*. From the pleasures of sleeping beneath the stars, to makeshift shelters.

William Golding: *Lord of the Flies* (Faber and Faber Ltd, 2004).
The true nature of man living apart from society in the absence of laws and morals, when the survival instinct has taken over. All the more striking as it is from the viewpoint of 12-year-old children shipwrecked on an island.

Italo Calvino: *The Baron in the Trees* (Thomson Learning, 1977).
Having climbed into his oak at twelve years of age, the young Cosimo di Rondo does not set foot on the ground again. This philosophical fable has influenced a whole generation of amateur builders of tree houses.

Henry David Thoreau: *Walden; or Life in the Woods* (Dover Publications, 1995).
Day-to-day life as experienced by Henry David Thoreau, American essayist in self-imposed exile and isolation in a cabin in the heart of the woods.

Michel Tournier: *Vendredi ou les Limbes du Pacifique [Friday or Limbo in the Pacific]* (Gallimard, 1967). Robinson Crusoe revisited with psychoanalysis by a present-day French novelist.

Marc-Antoine Laugier: *Essai sur l'Architecture* (1753), (Liège, éd. Mardaga, 1979).

Le Corbusier: *Une Maison, un Palais: à la Recherche d'une Unité Architecturale* (Paris, éd. Connivences, coll. de l'Esprit nouveau, 1989).

Philosophical works

Jean-Jacques Rousseau: *Émile* (Phoenix mass market, 1993).

Gaston Bachelard: *La Terre et les Rêveries de la volonté. Essai sur l'Imagination de la Matière*, (José Corti, 1992).

Martin Heidegger: 'Building, Dwelling, Thinking', in *Poetry, Language, Thought*, trans. Albert Hofstadter (Harper Colophon Books, 1971).

Didier Anzieu: *L'Enfant et sa Maison*
(éd. ESF, 1988).

A thesis

Karine Aillerie: 'Les robinsonnades', M Phil thesis, under M. Castillo, Université d'Angers, 1994.

Other books on cabins

Joseph Ryjkwert: *On Adam's House in Paradise: the Idea of the Primitive Hut in Architectural History* (The MIT Press, 1981).

Art Boericke and Barry Shapiro: *Handmade Houses: A Guide to the Woodbutcher's Art* (A & W Pub, 1985).

Concerning emergency and temporary housing

Donald McDonald: *Democratic Architecture: Practical Solutions to Today's Housing Crisis* (Whitney Library of Design, 1996).

Robert Kronenburg: *Houses in Motion: The Genesis, History and Development of the Portable Building* (Academy Ed., 1995).

Some websites

www.lerecoursauxforets.org
French language website with no fuss and plenty of information and stories of all kinds. You can download an extract of the film *Éloge de la Cabane (Eulogy to the Cabin)* referred to above, and meet the 'cabannoniers', men and women who devote their lives to their cabins: 'In the cabin you don't have to do anything else but be as happy as possible.'

www.sitewan.org/cabanes
General information site (in French, with some English content) with a strong emphasis on keeping its information, texts and changes as up to date as possible.

archilibre.free.fr
Personal site of Jean Soum, professor of architecture and great builder of cabins (French site, but with full English version).

vagabondart.org/cabanes.htm
Gives access to sites covering art and sociology, with technical files and personal stories (French site).

A documentary film
Robin Hunzinger: *Éloge de la Cabane [Eulogy to the Cabin]*, a 52-minute documentary, made in 2003. Produced by Bruno Florentin. Music: Jean-Philippe Chalté. Production: Real Productions. Distribution: Dix Francs. 8, rue Lamartine, 75008 Paris.
A poetic vision of games and sensory experiences in connection with cabins. Starting with his own experiences of a cabin, in the Vosges, Robin Hunzinger goes on to tell of others who have constructed their own cabins in other regions of France.

photographic credits

Corbis *Paul Almasy 47 – Archives du Canada/Sygma 70 – Luca Babini 29 – Dave Bartruff 72-73 – Bettmann 34, 44, 82-83, 93 – Michael Busselle cover 1 verso, 54-55 – Corbis 71 – Richard Cummins 63 – Vander Zwalm Dan 10-11 – Pagani Flavio 49 – Owen Franken 51, 52-53, 66-67 – Hulton-Deutsch Collection 69 – Wolfgang Kaehler 48 – David Katzenstein 60-61 – Layne Kennedy 4 – Chris Lisle 57 – Gunter Marx Photography 3rd cover – Massimo Listri 9t, 12-13 – David Muench 28 – Charles O'Rear cover 1 recto. – Carl & Ann Purcell 56, 68 – David Samuel Robbins 75 – Leonard de Selva 36-37 – Stapleton Collection 18 – Peter Turnley 42 – Ruggero Vanni 13 – Jacques-Édouard Vekemans 6-7 – Patrick Ward 62, 64-65.*
Masterfile *Gary Rhijnsburger 4th cover, 8, 14-15 – Richard Smith 16-17.*
Léon Mazzella *1.*
André Morin *20 Le Carré rouge, Gloria Friedmann, Villars-Santenoge (52), © André Morin & le consortium Dijon.*
Philippe Vaurès *Santamaria 9, 19, 21t, 29t, 30-31, 32-33, 38, 39, 40, 41, 50-51, 74, 78-79, 80-81.*

acknowledgements

Thanks to the following architects, artists and designers for their help:
Asymptote pour Knoll International p. 24-25 A3, **© Knoll International.**
Atelier Van Lieshout p. 43 *Favela-Beach House, © courtesy of AVL – p. 42t, 45, 101, 102 Favela- AVL ville, © courtesy of AVL – p. 46 Favela-Barcelone, © courtesy of AVL – p. 21b Autocrat (artwork), © courtesy of AVL – p. 94-95 Bais-O-Drome, © courtesy of AVL – p. 95 Maxi Capsule Luxus (artwork), © courtesy of AVL – p. 96-97 Star Wagon, © courtesy of AVL (www.ateliervanlieshout.com).*
Shigeru Ban p. 27 *Paper Longhouse (Kobe, Japon, 1995), © Philippe Magnon, Collection Fonds Régional d'Art Contemporain du Centre, Orléans, France.*
Ronan and Erwan Bouroullec p.22-23 *Cabane Kreo, © Morgane Legall, (courtesy galerie KREO, Paris, France) – p. 86-87 Lit clos (version petit modèle), © Marc Domage, (courtesy galerie KREO, Paris, France) – p. 26 Air house (exhibited at Villa Noailles, France), © Ronan and Erwan Bouroullec.*
La Cabane perchée p. 9, 40 *Cabane perchée, © Philippe Vaurès Santamaria (www.la-cabane-perchee.com).*
Collectif Inflate p. 84, 85 *Inflation sequences, © courtesy of Collectif Inflate.*
Matali Crasset p. 34t, 35 *Permis de construire (2000), © Patrick Gries, ed. Domeau & Pérès (http://www.domeauperes.com) – p. 75t, 93, p. 92-93 Oritapi (1999), © Patrick Gries, ed. Domeau & Pérès – p. 22, 98-99 Red cell (2001), © Yves Brunner & Alex Krassovski – p. 76-77 Popup space (2002), © Corinne Cuendet, musée de Design et des Arts appliqués contemporains, Lausanne, Switzerland (http://www.matalicrasset.com).*
Vincent Dupont-Rougier and Patrick Nadeau p. 88-89 *Meuble-jardin, © Christophe Fillioux (http://vdr.free.fr; patricknadeau.com).*
Christophe François for Kasane p. 24 *Lounge mobile, © Kasane.*
Lucy Orta p. 90-91 *Refuge Wear-Habitent (1992/3) Aluminium coated polyamide, telescopic armature, lamp and whistle, © Galerie Anne de Villepoix (www.studio-orta.com).*
And many thanks to Bruno Degoul, editorial assistant.

Every effort has been made to obtain the necessary rights and permissions. The publisher should be notified of any errors or omissions and these will be corrected in subsequent editions.